I CA... I SURVIVED

My first two days of working for the Preble, Humboldt, Bellevue, Scott, New Franken and Eton School District in August of 1960, were confusing, terrifying, and seemed to last as long as that name. I plotted methods of escape in the few spare moments we had. Could I just go home and take the job in Menominee that my father — without asking — interviewed for on my behalf? The annual salary offer he got was $3,900, $200 less than what I would receive at Preble, and my brother and his friends would be members of the student body, a fate I was sure would be worse than any I currently might be facing.

The possibility of eloping to Texas where my fiancé was stationed was out of the question, because he was sure "no one would approve," and I "probably would never get another job." There had to be some way I could avoid coming face to face with six classes of sophomore and junior English students in five days on the Tuesday after Labor Day.

I got lost on Thursday on my way to in-service. Even though I had practiced the route to school I turned left at three corners and ended up on Willow Street...wherever that was. I pulled into a gas station in my two-tone blue, Nash Rambler American which I had bought with a a down payment of $5.00 two weeks before. My frantic request for directions brought a look of amusement to the faces of several old-timers, gathered for coffee and probably to discuss the new coach, Vince Lombardi, and the Packers chances for the year.

"You can't hardly get there from here," was their first response but seeing the look of despair on my face they gave it a try and I actually arrived just a few minutes after 8 am.

After finding my way to the office I was greeted by two smiling women who informed me that they had just spoken to my mother in Menominee, Mich. She assured them I was on my way and they directed me to the library down the hall.

Stepping up to the double doors, I noted a tall, balding man standing at the podium with his back to me. The rest of the staff — 35 people I later learned — stared at the tardy newcomer frantically trying to spot an empty chair. All of the tables appeared to be occupied and the only opening, at least that I could get to, was in a middle seat on a couch to the right of the door. I sidled in as quietly as I could, considering I was wearing a charm bracelet that jingled with every step I took, and sank down between two suited gentlemen who smiled congenially. Actually, everyone was smiling — maybe smirk would be a better word. I soon recognized the speaker as John David, the superintendent who had interviewed with me in the spring. He waited until I was seated and then proceeded to introduce the administration, beginning with Principal Peter Hamel. The man on my left stood. Next was Vice-Principal Ed Blecha and the man on my right stood. By the time he got to the new staff and introduced Miss Meissner, an English teacher, I knew my first day as a Hornet would not soon be forgotten.

Between sessions, during which we listened to such subjects as the "philosophy of education as adopted by the unified school district," we were allowed to go to our rooms to prepare. Having received my list of students and rooms I discovered that no two classes were in the same room and if they had been I would not have known where it was. I wandered the halls and watched people industriously lining up desks and placing books on shelves. Finally, as I was about ready to make a run for it, a nice man introduced himself and invited me into his room. He turned out to be George Bradley, the head of the English Department, and he asked if he could help.

He first located the nearest classroom I would be using during another teacher's prep period and we discovered there were no English books on the shelves. After traveling both floors, from a social studies room on the second floor north to the chorus on the first floor south, we located a cart and began to haul literature and grammar books, neither of which I had ever laid eyes on. This accomplished, he sat me down and talked me through the first chapter of literature.

Having opened in 1955, Preble was only five years old and already suffering growing pains. There were no spare rooms for new teachers. I would be expected to keep my classes orderly and the room neat.

On Friday afternoon we gathered in the cafeteria to listen to various speakers, one of them a physical education/science teacher who reported on the Welcome Back Dinner the Board of Education sponsored each fall. Seated next to me was the librarian, Lucy Groffer. As I sat and listened to the handsome gentleman she whispered, "He's our most eligible bachelor. Get him!" She, of course, did not realize I was still plotting an elopement to Texas. I often wonder what that very wise lady would say if she knew that the "eligible bachelor" and I were married for 57 years.

Entering the faculty room at the end of the day I was looking forward to hopping into my car and heading for home.

"Psst," loudly whispered a redheaded, female, physical education teacher from across the room. "Wanna go for a beer?"

I had turned 21 the previous November, so I thought I might as well meet my co-workers and I headed to the Fern Room with Helen Harrison, fellow Mount Mary alum Bette Drossart, and Betty Dunne, the chorus teacher. There we met Gene Hall, the aforementioned

4

eligible bachelor, Doug Lueck, another newcomer to Preble, a few others I don't recall. I got through the weekend, resisted the temptation to make a run for it, and survived my first day in the classroom. I even made it through the class of 34 juniors held in the chorus room, sandwiched between the band room and the gym, and across from the cafeteria-- during second lunch period. Many days that first year C. Scott Hunsberger, the band instructor, and one of my favorite people, would hurry in after class and challenge me to "name the tunes" they had played that hour. It was beginner's band. Reunions in following years brought tales of mischief that surrounded that class...some of which I firmly believe were products of junior Wally Proski's imagination.

Many students I had that year were only four or five years younger than I, and I know now that I learned a lot more than they did. Our children grew up together. We cheered at soccer matches and attended the same school events. We are invited to class reunions and I have been forever grateful that I showed up that first day!

WHO CALLED THAT PLAY?

Some of my favorite memories of those first years at Preble High School, were related to Saturday afternoon football games at Preble Park. Before sharing City Stadium with East High, and then finally building Gauthier Stadium on the old Zimonick cornfield across from the school, the Hornets played their Northeast Wisconsin Conference games at the windy, and often chilly park on Hillside Lane. The conference was strong and the games were exciting. The last game of the season they played against East De Pere, always a big rival, and a win for either would mean a share of the conference championship.

On this particular Saturday the game was tied, and the clock was running as Preble moved the ball down the field. The Hornets were out of time-outs and after a run, which moved them closer to the goal, the players returned to their respective huddles, with the exception of one Hornet who was sprawled on the field. Dr. George Herring, team physician, hurried to check the injury. He called for help to move him to the sideline and ultimately to his car. This, of course, gave coaches Jerry Dufek and Bill Dessart more time to come up with a plan. The game ended with a Preble touchdown and they tied with Sturgeon Bay.

As Ethel Dufek and I left the field, we watched the very excited Hornets board their bus. As it left the parking lot, we were startled to see the Principal of East De Pere run to kick the vehicle as it passed.

At the post game celebration in the school cafeteria, we laughed as Doc Herring told his story. He said he almost had a heart attack while driving, when the injured player sat up in the back of the wagon and asked, "How did I do?"

A week later my husband and I drove to Milwaukee to attend the annual teacher's convention. As we walked into the bar of the Schroeder Hotel, a must stop to see who had attended the convention, we were surprised to hear that same principal loudly proclaiming that De Pere was robbed of the victory. At the time I was a bit disgusted. As I look back, after observing years of football at all levels, I am amused as I realize that he was probably right...not that I think De Pere would have handled it any differently had the tables been turned.

(Coaches Dufek and Dessart)

A LAMB IN SHEEP'S CLOTHING

When I moved to Green Bay in fall of 1960 my social life was limited to high school football games, parent-teacher conferences and an occasional teacher gathering. It picked up when I joined a bowling league at North Side Lanes. I met a group of older, interesting women, and I got a kick out of reporting that I had bowled a 99 pin game against Lowie Herber, wife of Packer great Arnie. My sponsor, the Zuider Zee Supper Club, appreciated me for my handicap.

We hadn't been bowling long when my teammates, more experienced than I in Green Bay nightlife, decided I needed to be shown around. I reluctantly agreed. We began the adventure on Adams Street at the Mayfair Lounge, which they assured me was the hot spot with great entertainment. As we approached the Northland Hotel, my guides Bunny and Val began to laugh and turned to give me my first lesson of the evening. "See that man standing in front of the revolving door?" they asked. "When you pass him you must say, 'Hi there, Mr. Chauffer.' Get it right or he will correct you and ask you to repeat it." They shouted out the greeting and I echoed it somewhat reluctantly, because as I studied the little man in his formal grey coat and driver's hat I remembered who he was.

I had often traveled with my parents and grandparents on shopping and entertainment trips to Green Bay from our home in

Upper Michigan. When we spotted the man known as Mr. Chauffeur, my usually proper, paternal grandmother would mutter "That damn fool," and we would cross the street. Eventually my mother explained that he was Grandma's half -brother who had estranged himself from the family.

I'd run across him on occasion over the years and was told by locals that he had been paid by his family to stay away, information I knew to be untrue. When I passed him at his post at the Northland I'd call out the requisite greeting but I really, really wanted to say, "Hi there, Great-half-uncle Freddie!" I always wondered how he would have reacted.

In later years the Lindsleys, friends who lived downtown, told of meeting him as they walked with their children. He would put his hand up to his ear and they would shout out, "Hi there, Mr. Chauffeur!" and he would hand out candy treats.

After he passed on, I attended a retreat on Chambers Island and several of us visited the lighthouse. My mother always said that Grandma was born in Door County but she thought it was on Washington Island. We had never been able to find proof of that. That day, as we descended from the light tower, I was stopped in my tracks by a picture of Mr. Chauffeur posted next to a genealogy of my grandmother's family. The Williams had been both fishermen and lumbermen and they had sold the land for the lighthouse to the government around 1870 for $250. Grandma's uncles became the original lighthouse keepers. Her actual birthplace was Fish Creek and family members sometimes commuted to work on the island by traveling across the ice and even to Marinette to shop.

Fred Williams, alias Mr. Chauffeur, may have been estranged from his family but I can happily say that on that day he helped bring me together with mine. Sometimes a black sheep is, in reality, just a little gray lamb.

Mr. Chauffer   Age 39
King of all Highways   21 years
without an accident

BEWARE THE TALES OF THE IRISH

As an English major in college I was fortunate to have Sr. Cornelius as one of my professors. She was a Notre Dame nun, Irish, and a great storyteller. At school newspaper meetings she would occasionally drink from a can of beer, wrapped in a brown bag, which someone had brought her from Malone's Corner Drug Store. At the end of the year Sigma Tau Delta Banquets for English majors, we bought her favorite cocktail served in a coffee cup. She also had a cupboard full of mystery stories that she unlocked to show me, and promised I could pick out a good read when I needed a break. I am sure some of that closeness came from the fact that her good friend was my high school principal who had joined me, Mary St. Peter and Mary Staudenmaier, as we all moved from Lourdes High School to Mount Mary College.

On a slow or gloomy day, when Ben Johnson or Samuel Pepys was putting us to sleep, she would launch into one of her tales of "the little people of Ireland." As we listened and chuckled she would warn us, "Be careful! Non-believers and those who disrespect are in for trouble!" We, of course, snickered and brushed aside the warnings. The only thing that could save us, she promised, was a primrose, as that flower could ward off the evil.

As I began my first year of teaching at Preble High School, I would find that my small, last period, class of juniors often became restless. Reading to them or telling stories kept them from misbehaving, especially on Friday afternoon. I eventually began repeating Sr. Cornelius' stories and most of the class became spellbound. They reacted as I had when I first heard them and were ready for more. One young man in particular got caught up in the adventures and egged me on, scorning the warnings I put forth.

Homecoming that first year was the last game of the season, the last weekend in October. This was before the administration figured out that if it were scheduled early in the year there was a lot less time for the students to plan mischief. My roommate, Sharon, a history teacher at St. Joseph Academy, and I visited the houses where the sophomores and juniors were busily building floats. The juniors were at Bonnie Dollar's and after we saw that they were almost done, we moved on to a big lot on Bader and Hillside where the sophomores were gathered. We were not there long before Mitch, who liked the stories, showed up waving a fake yellow primrose in my face. I was impressed that he had taken the time and trouble to find it and we all had a good laugh. I assured him that it was a smart move.

The following week was teacher's convention, my first, and I drove to Milwaukee to meet and stay with Hellen Walker, a college friend who taught in the city. Before heading home I stopped at

Mount Mary and visited with Dean Celine, sharing some of my new experiences. By the time I bypassed Green Bay and arrived at my parent's home in Menominee, it was rather late and Mother said Sharon had called and I was supposed to return her call as soon as I could. She wanted to talk to me before I saw the news as Mitch had been killed in an accident the night before on Willow Street, near the Zuider Zee, a popular restaurant. I still remember how terrible I felt and I could not escape the picture of him, waving the yellow flower or my assuring him that he was now safe. I knew the Irish little people were not really to blame…the police said excessive speed was the cause…but I could not help feeling guilty and dreaded meeting his class on Monday. As I expected they were very quiet, and Sandy, who had been dating him, was angry. I never again told the stories and now I sometimes regret that I have forgotten them.

Although the events of the following story take place 40 years after
this one, they share the theme of Gaelic tales and stir the imagination.

COULD A FAIRY RING FIASCO FOSTER
TERRORIST ATTACKS?

(A fairy ring is a wooded site in Ireland where fairies romp)

"And you must walk four times, counter clockwise, around the fairy ring," warned Jerry, manager of Castledaly Manor.

"Why four times?" questioned my niece, Kristin, a bit cynical in regard to fairy ring rules.

Unable to get an acceptable response, we trudged out into the damp, darkening woods surrounding the ivy-covered manor house. Following treasure map type directions, we marched past two large, gray stones, beyond a moss-covered log, and then turned right into the trees. In single file we followed a narrow, worn path toward a circle of fallen limbs. Climbing over the barrier, four of us obediently began the requisite counter clockwise laps. Meanwhile Jill, unmindful of the wrath of Gaelic little people, set about tying Kleenex "ghosts" to overhanging branches. Snapshots of these were meant to provide Cade, her four -year old son back in Sun Prairie, with evidence of Irish haunts.

Having finished our laps Mary, Lisa, Kris and I proceeded to snap pictures of the peculiar arrangement of branches woven into a circle approximately twenty feet in diameter, reminiscent of a tornado's aftermath.

Back in the manor house, as we waited for dinner, we reported our activities to fellow travelers. Manager Jerry recoiled in horror at our boldness and failure to exercise proper precautions.

"You took pictures in the fairy ring?" he shouted! "The last person who did that lost his room key and his passport!" We snickered, assuming, of course, that he was pulling our legs with more Irish hyperbole. "Laugh," he scoffed, "but wait until tomorrow. You will be running around stark naked!" Unable to pinpoint the relationship, this brought more guffaws.

"I guarantee," he proclaimed, shaking a finger in an ominous gesture, "your plane will never take off on time!" Well that would not be the first time that happened, so we figured the pictures and the fake ghosts were worth a few extra minutes in the beautiful country family members, with County Claire heritage, had been touring for eight days. It may be worth mentioning that Margaret, Chelsea, and I had already experienced the presence of spirits that supposedly made Castledaly the most haunted manor house.

At breakfast the next morning, August 14, 2006, Tom mentioned hearing a CNN report regarding an incident at London's Heathrow. Words like "terrorist threat" and "no planes would fly from London to the U4S" were spoken but we went about packing a bus that would take us from Athelone to the airport. Upon arrival in Dublin we noticed the presence of a large contingent of armed security forces that had not been there when we flew in, but it was not until we got to the boarding area that we realized the effect the "London incident" would have.

"No lotions, no gels, no lipstick and no $40 Irish whiskey would be allowed in carry-ons. Scrambling to find the most available space, we ended up stashing most of our forbidden items in bags Chelsea and Sarah would check.

Grim-faced, but calm and efficient airport personnel, moved about determined and yet reassuring. Passengers began to arrive at the Aer Lingus terminal telling stories about early morning flights they had already flown from London. A tiny baby was boarded with his mom on the second of four flights he would take before reaching Vancouver, WA, long after the formula they carried would run out. No plane would fly directly from the UK to the US that day.

We watched a silly Chevy Chase vacation movie as we were repeatedly warned not to gather in groups as we waited for the restroom to become available.

Upon arrival at O'Hare, just 15 minutes behind schedule, flight attendants passed around plastic bags holding confiscated belongings and we pulled out our cells to talk with family who had remained in Wisconsin. We were surprised to hear that they had spent the day glued to the news stations or fielding calls from others who worried that 13, yes 13, family members would not return home on time.

So let the truth be known! When you board your next flight with all the liquids packed in two ounce bottles and stashed in plastic bags, it just might be because Jill and Kris and Lisa took pictures in an Irish fairy ring. Or maybe, just maybe, one of us walked only three times around the circle...clockwise!"

Sarah, Kris, Chelsea, Rick and Lisa wait at Dublin Airport after removing all liquids and gels from carry-ons.

FIVE YEARS ON FRANZ AVENUE

As we drove up to 1648 Franz Avenue, I noticed a lady peering from the doorway across the street.

"Oh, great, I thought. "She is probably the one who told Gene's mother about the rental and she is spying on us!"

Our wedding was six weeks away and we had no idea where we were going to live. This apartment sounded the most promising. It was downstairs, had three bedrooms and was not far from Preble High School where we would both be teaching. The rent was $70 a month provided we cut the grass and shovel the snow. Otherwise it would be $75. After one walk through we met the owners, the Duquesne's, and signed a contract beginning what would be five years filled with memorable occasions, both good and heartbreaking.

Much of the land in the town of Preble was owned and farmed by the Zimonick family. Franz Avenue was a dead end street with George Zimonick living on the east end and Frank Zimonick Jr. and his wife Mary on the west end. Between the two of them there was seldom a dull moment... or person.

Strawberries ripened in spring calling for ice cream sundaes in George's back yard. Each fall neighborhood men rose before dawn to fire up the booyah kettle in Frank's front yard. Others peeled fresh corn and when it was time, lit the grills. But I am getting ahead of myself.

The summer before our August 19 wedding, Gene taught driver education and I roomed with Busy Fordyce, caring for the dogs that she and her roommate, Helen Harrison owned. Besides working on wedding plans, I attempted to play golf with Louise Criel. One day Louise called quite early in the morning…the dogs and I preferred to sleep later. She said she couldn't wait because her friend Dorrie Henquinet had called and asked if we wanted to golf with her neighbor, Cherry Starr, wife of Packer quarterback Bart. I was willing to make a complete fool of myself to be able to say I had done that and I must say she was very understanding. At one point I hit the ball about five feet…sideways, and it grazed her cart. She handed me an old, beaten up ball she had picked up along the way and proclaimed, "You really slammed that one!"

On weekends we returned to Franz Avenue to measure curtains, line cupboards and cut the grass…well we tried. The first time Gene went out with the lawn mower I heard shouting and ran to the kitchen door in time to see a large, dark-haired man shove the mower under the porch.

"In this neighborhood the women cut the grass, "he shouted. This was my first experience of the antics of John Harrington who lived three houses to the west.

We had met Marge and John and were made aware of his eccentricities by Jerry and Ethel Dufek. Jerry was a science teacher at Preble and a varsity football coach. They and their three children, Kim, Tina and Craig, lived across from Frank. John had played professional football for the Cleveland Browns and when he moved to Green Bay, he drove into Jahnke's gas station to request that the air in his tires be replaced with fresh Wisconsin air. Jahnkes, who also lived on Franz Avenue, wondered about their new neighbor.

When we returned from our honeymoon in August, we were happy to see that Pranges had delivered our furniture and we settled in, anticipating a few quiet days to get organized before school started. But first we had to clean. Len Kazmer, Jerry Dufek and Doug Lueck had come calling. We found condoms hanging from the light fixtures, water on the floor, rice scattered from the kitchen to the bedroom and a very unsanitary bathroom. I remember being down on my hands and knees and hearing car horns signifying a wedding party. My thought was…enjoy it now, fools! In a week you will be scrubbing floors! Later that week we went out to sit on the porch and were joined by John and Carol Smith who lived upstairs. We had not been there long when firecrackers began exploding and a crowd of people appeared banging on pots and pans.

Unfamiliar with shivaree protocol, Gene and I just sat, our

mouths hanging open. Ted Criel, who had stood up for our wedding, was a Rahr's beer distributor and he stepped up to assure us that his truck was parked around the corner and we were supposed to say "We will buy the beer!" Coworkers and neighbors supplied the food and sometime during the party managed to short sheet our bed. When we woke up in the morning we discovered Doug asleep on our couch.

The Van Stratens lived just east of us, on George's end. Ray and Elsie were great neighbors. Ray was very knowledgeable about cars and comforted Gene when our 1963 Ford died at an early age. He reassured him that it was okay. Teachers couldn't know everything-- like cars need oil to run. He never again missed an oil change.

Our daughter Lisa was born in May of 1962, and Elsie and Esther Malcore, Grandma's friend from across the street, became loving watchdogs for her first five years.

The Harrington's moved to Quincy Street to accommodate their growing family and the Krause's moved in. I had two of their children in homeroom and they all babysat for us. Rosalie Hanson, from Frank's side of the street, also a student of mine, was "super sitter." Her boyfriend scolded me because she always checked to see if we needed her before accepting a date.

The Rossmeissls were in the middle of the block. John was the Green Bay Superintendent of Mails. He hunted and one year he cooked bear stew for the neighbors.

The Sylvesters, across the street, had Mike and Suzy and taught me that you don't just invite one kid from a family to a birthday party. Dumb me thought 3 year old Lisa's party would just be for girls…I went to a Catholic school and you didn't mix until at least eighth grade! Next door to them were the DeGroots, and I spent five years trying to decide which girl I was speaking with… Laurie, Lida, Lana, Lola or Luanne.

There were no crops to harvest in Green Bay in the winter but George Zimonick decided that an off-season block party was called for. He had heard that a restaurant in St. Anna, a small village 50 miles south of Green Bay, bought top of the line steaks from Frankenthal's packing plant so he rented a bus to get us all there. Imagine our surprise when we boarded, and found our assistant pastor from St. Phillip's Church, dressed in his black suit and a white cocktail apron serving as the designated bartender.
The steaks were great and we had a wonderful time. George thoughtfully offered to pay to repair the phone line that our bus knocked down on Main Street.

My most embarrassing moment on Franz Avenue occurred one noon hour. Pushing Lisa in her stroller I walked to Super Value just across Main Street. As I passed Oak Grove School, the children were coming out and I noticed a man sitting in his car, hat pulled down on his head, watching them closely. When I returned home he was still there so I called the police and suggested that they check him out… and they did. He was Mr. Everard, the school principal, who did noon duty sitting in his car.

The saddest days of those five years occurred on the three occasions when we lost a daughter, after Lisa was born beautiful and healthy. The first baby, I think of her as Cynthia, was full term but because my blood was RH negative, we were incompatible and the baby was stillborn. The other two were at various stages of development when they stopped breathing. Each time, Ethel Dufek, my thoughtful friend, preceded me wherever we went to explain why I was no longer wearing maternity clothes, but had no infant. After Christmas, 1968, we made a decision to begin adoption proceedings as

well as the search for a home of our own. With the help of "the spy", Esther Malcore, we found the perfect house. They had toured but it was too big for them. Our deed says the house was

1648 Franz Ave.

built on land that was originally Zimonick gardens.

As much as I hated to leave all of our friends and neighbors, it was a new beginning to help erase some of the sad memories. Lisa was unhappy at first as she now had to walk six blocks to school instead of the half block she would have traveled but her attention was diverted somewhat by the arrival of her baby brother in February of 1969. We had one big reunion party at our new house, but the atmosphere in our finished basement was different from that experienced in the Zimonicks' yards. The neighborhood ladies birthday club met for lunch for years but we are now down to three. Louise Kazmer, Joanne Rossmeissl and Jane Carpenter are gone. Ethel, Marge Harrington and I are left to recall many fond memories.

WHAT'S IN A NAME?

"Archie Moore," my husband declared as he looked at a hospital picture of our brand new baby girl.

"Archie Moore, the boxer?" I screamed. You think this beautiful baby looks like Archie Moore?" It wasn't his first mistake of the day.

On May 23, 1962, I sat typing a final exam on Julius Caesar for the substitute teacher who had recently taken over my English classes. Somewhere between "Et Tu Brute" and "Friends, Romans, Countrymen, lend me your ear," twinges of pain began to nag. I squeezed in a couple phone calls to more experienced friends and they assured me that this was probably it.

After a long night of cribbage and a brief nap or two we left for the hospital at 5:30 AM on Thursday, May 24, and continued the discussion that had been going on for months. If the baby was a boy, he would be named Daniel Gene Hall after his dad and great grandfather, but should it be a girl no agreement had been reached.

I wanted Hillary, Hillary Hall. After all, my old friend had named her child Pamela Poletti and I had been Mary Meissner, Menominee, Michigan. It worked for me. "It has to be a square name!" Gene insisted. My college roommates thought the answer was obvious. She should be Caroline Hall, our dorm at Mount Mary

College. The President's daughter was Caroline and I was afraid many new mothers would make that choice.

After spending the next five hours, breathing heavily and listening to the radio tell of the misadventures of the landing of NASA's Project Mercury, I was rushed to the delivery room with little time to spare. Hoping for natural childbirth with no meds and a mirror to watch the entrance of my first baby, I groaned in despair as Dr. Guthrie ran into the room and ordered, "Put her out!" And out I went. I awoke later to find a woman washing her hands in the sink adjacent to the table upon which I lay.

"How's Scott Carpenter?" I asked and she rushed to my side responding, "It's a lovely name, dear, but your baby is a girl!"

"No, No, the astronaut. He was lost when I came in here," and off she ran to get the latest news. Returning she reassured me that Carpenter had landed and had been recovered safely after overshooting his target by 250 miles. Ready to be reunited with my family, she then wheeled me to recovery passing my husband and Dr. G standing in the hall. "Now will you help me think of a girl's name?" I pleaded. Dr. G stepped up to say that you have to have a girl first to help with the dishes. Just what a budding feminist and recent graduate of all women's college wanted to hear!

We finally agreed to name her after her mother and great

grandmother, and the beautiful baby girl when home from the hospital with us. One week later, a letter appeared in the People's Forum of the Green Bay Press Gazette, scolding men who do not support their wives when they have baby girls instead of boys. I knew exactly to whom she was speaking, even though her assumption was not really correct. It was written and signed by the nun who was the head of the obstetrics department of St. Vincent Hospital. It was written by the woman who helped deliver my child and who had escorted me from the delivery room, and she was talking to my husband and my doctor. I wish I had kept the letter. It would have been a great addition to Mary Elizabeth's baby book.

Is she happy with her name? Well, we ended up calling her Lisa, probably the most popular name of that year, far more than Caroline, but Lisa Hall was a perfectly square name and she says at least she doesn't sound like a dorm.

WANNA SEE MY BIRD?

"How would you like a green and yellow parakeet complete with all the trimmings?" asked neighbor, Ethel Dufek. "My mother gave it to us and my kids are afraid of it."

As we had just given our dog away, we accepted. A bird seemed a more apartment friendly pet for a two and a half year old. Lisa often entertained herself by pulling up a kitchen chair to talk to him. Pete's response was a screech that increased in volume when I found her poking a stick into the cage to make the bird jump from one perch to another. Her screams of laughter brought me running. After lectures on animal cruelty she would stop for a bit or at least she would wait until I was on the phone or engaged in another pursuit.

Guests who entered the house were immediately hustled to the kitchen to meet Pete. Two of these occasions stand out.

Each Christmas Ted Fritsch donned a beautiful red velvet suit and made the rounds taking orders and giving out small gifts. Ted played running back for the Packers from 1942 till 1950, and he looked the part of the "jolly old man!" My husband refereed high school football with him and we felt fortunate to be added to his stops. In the past we had gathered friends at Helen Harrison's home, but this year Lisa was recovering from chicken pox, so he bravely offered to come to our house. As Santa knelt to speak with her, Lisa leaned into him and asked, "Wanna see my bird?" After making the proper fuss over Pete, he gave her a gift from his bag and moved on. The following summer we took her to Bay Beach and as we prepared to board the miniature train, the gentleman serving as the engineer bent to her and asked, "How's your bird?" She didn't know about Santa's summer job.

The other occasion was not amusing. Our only experience with croup began around ten one cold, blustery night. Julie, the baby daughter of the couple who lived upstairs had died very suddenly of pneumonia several months before, and a distraught Dr. Hammes, who rushed to treat her, sat in my kitchen assuring me, and himself, that he had done all he could.

The horrible sound coming from my child was terrifying. We turned on the hot water and Gene sat with her while I called Dr. Guthrie. He called in a prescription and said he would come. Her breathing became easier while I waited, and I put her back in bed with the vaporizer and Vicks, and told her not to move as I went to admit the doctor. I opened the door to see a harried looking man who I was sure had left his warm bed. I turned to take him to the bedroom when I heard a little voice behind me rasp, "Wanna see my bird?"

"She doesn't seem that sick, was the immediate response" and I wanted to drop through the floor. Doc took a quick peak at Pete and checked out the kid. I explained about the little girl upstairs, whom his partner had cared for and he said that he too had thought of her immediately, although he did not realize she had lived upstairs.

Pete moved with us when we bought our home on Schober Street and his cage sat in the dining room where he could look out the window and watch the many birds congregating in four tall maples. Lisa, five when we moved, lost enthusiasm for her pet and when I told her I was writing about him her sole response was, "He pecked my nose!" One morning we found him lying at the bottom of his cage and we buried him in the traditional shoebox coffin soon to be forgotten by everyone but maybe Dr. Guthrie and Santa.

Santa with the Luecks, Criels, Dufeks, Cibulas and Lisa.

WE REALLY WERE AT THE ICE BOWL

I was meandering through the produce department of Albertson's grocery store in Temecula, CA, when I met a man, lurking between the strawberries and the sweet potatoes, hawking the local newspaper. He jumped out at me to ask if I would like a free copy of The Press Enterprise. I assured him that I had read it that morning and I would not need a subscription because I was visiting my son's family and would be returning home shortly.

"Where are you from?" he asked and when I responded Green Bay, Wisconsin, he asked the inevitable question, "And are you a Packer fan?" I gave my standard answer, "Yes, we have had tickets on the 40 yard line since the stadium was built"...both a bit of an exaggeration. They are actually on the 38 and I didn't get married and join my husband there until three years after it opened.

"Wow," he said, "were you at the Ice Bowl?" I assured him that I was and I could rattle off the facts. Date: Dec. 31, 1967. Temperature -15 with the wind chill of -36., Final score, Green Bay 21, Dallas 17. The Packers scored the winning touchdown on a quarterback sneak with Bart Starr following the blocking of Jerry Kramer and Ken Bowman.

Unfortunately, we have no tickets framed with pictures of us in game garb on our basement wall. We have those from three Rose

---

Bowls, and Super Bowl XXXII, but who knew we would need proof just because everyone who has ever driven past Lambeau Field claims they were at the game.

We didn't have phones that took selfies to post instantly. We had all we could do to dress for the cold. No time to worry about carrying a camera or snapping pictures. There wouldn't have been much to see anyway as we were clad in balaclavas and no would have recognized us. If your face wasn't covered with yarn, it was hidden by steam as the media pictures show.

The Ice Bowl Crowd

I don't remember what I wore. In later years we borrowed our neighbors' snowmobile suits. In the late 90's we just sold our tickets and stayed home to watch TV much to the dismay of our tailgating friends who declared us wimps.

I don't remember getting to the stadium, or where we parked the car, but I remember climbing to our seats in what was then section 17, row 42, a long way up when you can barely move. The 51,000 fans in attendance were all wider than they had been the previous game so we struggled to move in. A man behind us rudely shouted, "Just sit down!" I looked up, unable to see the face of the person, but I would have recognized the distinctive voice anywhere and I responded just as rudely," Shut up Virgil." Needless to say Virgil Valitchka was a bit surprised to find that behind the masks were the Halls, patrons of The Fern Room, his bar on Pine Street. Gene and I had been formally introduced there the first day I came to teach at Preble and we usually ended up there with friends to celebrate home victories. Virgil was a little embarrassed but we laughed and found seats nine and ten and settled in as best we could. At winter games you squeeze into your seat and wait to stand for the Star Spangled Banner. Before the last note dies away you sit down really fast so you get your share.

The UW La Crosse band was scheduled to play at halftime, but as they warmed up before the game the woodwinds froze and the player's lips stuck to their trumpets and trombones. We learned later that seven band members were taken to a local hospital to be treated for hypothermia and one elderly man died in the stands.

It wasn't long before we knew this was going to be a most

---

unusual game. The officials' whistles froze to their lips after the kickoff and they had to shout signals through torn and bloody skin for four quarters. It has been said that announcer Frank Gifford commented at one point, "I'm going to take a bite of my coffee now."

The Cuene's and the Nelson's always sat in the seats in front of us. While I had been a fan and listened to the Packers with my parents from a very early age, I was a rookie when it came to attending professional games and I sometimes said words that those around me considered inappropriate, like, "Just kick the field goal and let's get out of here. I'm freezing." They never seem to mind shivering during two timeouts called with 7 seconds to go to "ice the kicker." After receiving a few dirty looks, I learned to keep my opinions to myself. The day of the Ice Bowl I also learned to appreciate Vince who at third and goal with 16 seconds remaining told Bart, "Run it and let's get the hell out of here!" When an assistant asked what play they would use he responded "Damned if I know!" But Bart did and the quarterback sneak did the trick. While fans raced onto the field to tear down the goal posts, we "got out of there."

After the game we were invited to a party at the west side home of Wally and Lorraine Lambert. We followed directions to Leo Street and trailed behind the green and gold crowd entering a brick house. We didn't remove our coats as like most others we were still trying to get warm. Finally noticing that there were not many people we knew, we asked where our hosts were and discovered that the Lambert's lived next door.

I did not tell my story to the man in the store peddling the paper as I didn't want to spoil his idea that attending the Ice Bowl was the most thrilling experience anyone could ever have. It may be in retrospect, but at the time it was truly awful... but I sure wish I had my ticket in a frame for the basement archive so I can brag, fifty years later, that I really was at the Ice Bowl.

The winning touchdown

NINE GALLONS FOR MIKE

In the early seventies, I received a call from the special education office asking me to consider taking on a new homebound student who was a severe hemophiliac. Mike was the youngest in a family of three boys, all bleeders, and two girls, who could be carriers. The others had attended East Green Bay High School with some problems, but Mike's attendance was sporadic and he was struggling to keep up with his work. This was the beginning of a four-year assignment that was both heart warming and occasionally heart wrenching.

Mike's family members were wonderful people. His dad was a fireman and his mom worked part time for a local manufacturer. I was Mike's only teacher and I visited their home three days a week during the school year. There were interruptions in our schedule. If anyone in my family had any illness, I called to cancel. Any childhood disease, like chickenpox, could be life threatening for my student. There were weeks when I did not see him because of an issue he was dealing with. I remember hearing one Fourth of July that he fell from his bike returning from watching fireworks. His injuries, minor to most others, caused a major bleed requiring days of hospitalization and confinement to bed at home. Tooth decay was a fearful problem for him as was acne.

There was one week, in April of 1973, when Green Bay flooded and the water reached all the way to the railroad tracks on Webster Street adjacent to their home. It was on either flooded side. Mike's mom called to say, humorously, that I would not be able to reach them unless I could come by boat. I passed on that.

Mike was unbelievably positive and cheerful and we spent hours studying together. He was an ambitious student and took electives like Russian History. As an English major I especially enjoyed English Lit, and we became hilarious reading The Canterbury Tales in the original language. What fun it was to work with a young man who enjoyed learning even though he was deprived of the contributions of other students, and the fun of having friends in the classroom! We did have occasional family members and I loved it when his Dad was home. He was the cook, and the smell of freshly baked bread often permeated our kitchen classroom.

New "cures" for hemophilia would be found and the hopes of those around him would be raised. One in particular required them to buy a small refrigerator in which to store a medication that would be administered immediately if he suffered a bleed. It helped for a while.

Mike completed his high school years and went on to graduate from the University of Wisconsin- Green Bay with a BA in Business. I did not see him during this time but he never failed to send a

Christmas card and thanking me for the years we had worked together. I was happily surprised to run into him at the Automobile Association office where he was working as a travel agent but I was dismayed to see the pale young man, who had grown tall, but so much frailer than I remembered. One year I did not receive a card and soon his obituary was in the Press Gazette. This was all before news of the AIDS epidemic exploded and I could not help but wonder about the testing of all the donated blood that he had received.

After Mike graduated I began to realize the importance of blood donation to families like his, and I made my first trip to the Red Cross center on Deckner Avenue in a raging snowstorm. With a timeout for several years after breast cancer surgery, I continued to donate until I reached nine gallons and I was proud to display that number on my license plate. I do what I can to encourage others to donate, and I am sure that if they could experience the courage of people like Mike, they would do so. His brother passed away recently and when met I his wife she assured me that they all still remember those days.

FAPRI

Fifth Annual Pigboat Regatta Invitational

As we approached the Heath country home we observed ghostly figures appearing and then disappearing in the dense, grey fog. Once we entered the house they materialized into more familiar faces dressed in a wide variety of pre-regatta garb. This particular party, on Friday, August 17, 1979, was the now familiar prelude to the annual pigboat race. The souvenir program lists the committee as: Gary Whipp, Hugh and Marge Higley, Bob and Dina Meissner and Diane Wortner. The Meissners and the Higleys, both bay dwellers, had introduced the event five years earlier.

What on earth, you may ask, is a pigboat and who would race one? According to the plethora of information in the program, much of it a product of Bob's creative imagination, this type of competition was imported to the area by Cornish miners. A number of sailors, all male, were invited to attend. There was no established class of boat and rules were arbitrary. In our event the men ventured out in marginally sailable vessels called pigboats and ran a standard course. They returned to the starting position, drew a bottle of champagne from an inner tube (Blubby) and announced the name of their mate written on the bottle. After the partners downed the bubbly, the female completed the race…maybe. It is noted that eligibility requirements were loose so participants could continue to be invited back! All you needed was a sailboat, an entry fee, and a female companion. My experience with racing ended the next day, Saturday, August 18, at Helene Johnson's cottage on M35 in Menominee, Michigan.

My first year as a participant, 1975, at the Meissner home, was my best. Racing around the first buoy, I found myself on the inside and my nearest opponent, Patty Johnson, didn't make the turn. I was in first place and heading toward the finish line when I heard my partner, Gary Whipp, shouting at me, "Come toward me, Mary! Come toward me!' Unfortunately, the one aspect I'd never mastered when it came to sailing was coming about and as I turned toward him, instead of just heading to Escanaba as I had been doing, the boat capsized and I blew my chance. Who knows when I would have gotten back from "up north" but it might have been worth the trip!

That year J. Nason and M. Bowen went on to win in "Pig of my seart" and their names were the first engraved on the coveted trophy…a pig, on a boat, in a bottle. In 1976, Louanne Unks won with Gutzie in "Porcine Feather, and Chuck Heath and Helle sailed "Some Pig" to victory in 1977.

By 1979, I had gained somewhat of a reputation and no one went to the inner tube hoping to draw my name. Practice was in order and I went out with Bob's Sunfish accompanied by Debbie, Diane Whipp's daughter, who had taken to following me wherever I went. That ended when I dumped us both and she very loudly accused me of trying to drown her. I finally relaxed her grip on my neck and convinced her that the water was shallow enough for her to stand, but I doubt that she ever forgave or forgot.

One more attempt to practice the race route found me heading for the finish line when participant, George something or other (a rather crabby man whom I had never seen before or since) passed in front of me and I rammed his "brand new boat." I know this because he ranted about it the rest of the day. I truly did not see damage but I was afraid to get too close to look.

Needless to say by this time most of the male contingent was standing by Blubby pleading, "Please don't let me get Mary for my sailing partner." A few were actually saying it quite loudly. When the time came I panicked and shouted to my sister-in-law to take my place and she came through immediately. I knew she would not let me down. One of my favorite stories tells of a race in Door County when Bob and Dina were crewing. The boat keys fell into the water just as the race began and Dina stripped to her underwear and jumped in to recover them saving the day!

Over the years there were a lot of stories related to Pigboat and a lot of people attempted to cross that finish line. The Navy friends, Bob's fellow officers from the USS Long Beach, showed up on occasion and certainly added to the festivities. Weather was seldom a factor but one year the race was held at the Higley's and storms had flooded their lower level. We sat on a wall near the beach waiting fruitlessly for the waves to subside. The food was good and the company included Wally Lehman and his wife, Margot. They always added to my enjoyment.

Most of the races were held at Bob and Dina's. They purchased the home from our uncle, Archie Meissner, who had expanded it from a two-room cottage on M-35, to a split-level, four-bedroom home. Green Bay ebbed and flowed with the years and we were never sure whether we would be sitting on grass or out on the sand of the bay when the water had receded. At one time you traveled nearly a mile to the water where you could fish or boat. In later years they would awaken to find waves pounding on the windows and their lower level flooded.

I am not sure exactly when the event ended but it may have been ten years later. The race instigators moved…Bob into town where he said he felt like kissing the sidewalk every morning. The Higleys bought a home on the river where the threat of floods and storms were less stressful.

Once in awhile I come across the Fifth Annual Pigboat Regatta Invitational Souvenir Program in my scrapbook, or a picture or two I have kept, and I think, "If I had just kept sailing north my name would have been first on that coveted trophy!'"

Gene and Mary Lynn dressed in pre-race garb…sweats and "diamonds".

A LESSON LEARNED

I reached over and switched on the radio as I drove home in the dark. It had been a long day. I had begun my new job as a counselor at St. Joseph Academy just three weeks before and tonight had participated in an open house for eighth grade girls and their parents, a recruitment tool to add to our present enrollment of 622 students. The turn out had been encouraging.

I was enjoying the job. The counselor who had been there before me had left at the semester to join her husband in Colorado, and everyone said, "This is perfect for you. You will be there until you retire!" I had completed my master's program in August of 1982, and had only found part time employment in my field up until then. I liked my coworkers and my office looked out on a courtyard with trees. If you leaned out the window you could see the Fox River.

At nine-thirty, the easy listening station switched to local news and the first bit that captured my attention was an announcement that the Board of Education at Premontre, the all boys high school on the west side of Green Bay, had announced its intention to go coed-- details to follow at a later date. In just three weeks the promise of a job until retirement was suddenly not looking as good. That was February of 1985.

The transition was slow one and it wasn't until three years later

44

that Lynn, the Vice-Principal, and I sat in her office waiting for the Principal, Sr. Helen to return from a meeting with her superiors. When she finally arrived, the look on her face told us what we had not wanted to hear. With tears welling up in her eyes, she informed us that the Sisters of St. Joseph of Carondelet felt they could no longer provide sufficient religious staffing for all of their schools. Because there would be a Catholic high school alternative in Green Bay, we would be spending the next year shutting down the 94-year-old institution.

"What have I done wrong?" Helen asked. "This is the third school I've closed and I never thought it would happen to St. Joe's."

"It certainly wasn't anything you did," I tried to reassure her. She had graduated from the school as well as serving as its administrator. I knew she had worked hard to balance the books and encourage the faculty, some of whom were already starting to desert what they saw as a sinking ship. Maintaining enrollment was difficult as most eighth graders did not want to enter a school and then transfer before graduation.

The 1989-90 school year was a successful one in most ways. We awarded many scholarships and honors to graduate. We staged a host of farewell parties for students, staff, alumnae, board members and supportive community people who had been involved with SA. I met regularly with undergraduates in their classrooms to discuss their expectations and to share their sorrow, excitement and fear. Sr. Helen's goal, and consequently our goal, was to make the transition as easy as possible.

On Monday, March 12, 1990, I called to my husband as I was leaving for work, "This is probably going to be the worst week of my life." Driving through the dreary fog that often settled over the river, I thought about the letters that would arrive soon. Not all of us would be hired by the new Notre Dame Academy. Besides dealing with the students, I knew the staff would be in need of comfort and reassurance.

Little did I know how close my prediction would come. Leaving a classroom shortly before lunch, I came upon Lynn who had been searching for me. She dragged me into an empty room and told me of the horrendous accident that had taken place that morning on the Tower Drive Bridge. A mom of two of our students had been on the bridge and she did not survive. It was up to us now to find the girls and bring them to the office where family members waited. I had more than one lesson in my life that taught me perspective but none quite like the one I had that day. Life would go on for the staff and student body at the new school. Those of us who were not hired would find new jobs, some even better than the last one, but those two beautiful young girls wept and mourned for their mother and she could never be returned to them in their lifetime.

Fr. Gordon Gilsdorf and students burying a time capsule with memorabilia from each class, and Ann Hollenback's cookbook representing the staff, in the front yard, on one of the last days of the school.

.

WHEN ONE DOOR CLOSES.....

"I hate you! I hate you!" I walked around the Preble track repeating the words aimed at the principal of the new Catholic high school, the man who had not hired me. The brisk, April wind blew the ugly words behind me and helped to dry the tears that accompanied them. I had lost my job, the job that everyone thought would be there until I retired. I had only been working as a counselor at St. Joe's for five and one half years and the 94-year-old school was closing.

The long anticipated letters were sent to each staff member from the three merging schools to notify them regarding future employment. Mine arrived at my home while my son was on spring break and he called to tell me it was there. I asked him to open the letter and read paragraph four. Those who had already received theirs said that that was where you would find the key sentence. My family assured me that I would be hired but I heard the pause as he found the right place. "We will not be needing your services at this time but we thank you for your interest in Notre Dame Academy."

I had been on staff for a short time, but I had put in many extra hours and I felt I had worked hard. I would go in during the summer and on weekends to tour parents and students who were moving to Green Bay. We had recruitment nights and special weekend events to attract grade school girls.

It was a difficult time for all of us as the first question everyone asked was, "Well, did you get a job at the new school?" To make matters even worse, the president of the school board was quoted in the paper as having said, "All the qualified people were given jobs." Is that what she really said? I'd like to think not. The principal, supposedly trained in the correct way to merge schools, sent out invitations to all of the counselors in the area inviting them to apply for a position. They, in turn, rushed to me to ask what that was all about. I had no answer...must have been part of his "training". Staff members came to me to ask for help in writing resumes and cover letters. I did so willingly but could not write my own.

Yelling on an empty track was cathartic, but there were numerous social occasions involved with the closing and so many of us, including the students, were hurting. The accident on the Tower Drive Bridge occurred in April and the death of a mother of two students put things in perspective. A chance meeting with a priest who worked at Abbot Pennings, the boy's school also closing, was helpful as he assured me that "the principal was a man with a budget" and he could hire three people in place of our vice-principal and myself. That made it less of a personal issue but I laugh no thinking that it would have been a very low salary.

The one counselor who was hired had worked at Pennings for a long time and I would have hired her too. The two of us had often conferred. She only stayed at the new school one semester.

That spring my husband retired after 32 years of teaching and we were required to attend even more activities. The standard greeting was always, "I suppose you are going to Notre Dame."

We decided to replace a high mileage car and as we sat in the dealership the salesman asked us what we did. My husband responded, "I just retired," and I quietly replied that I was currently seeking employment. I was afraid he would not sell us a car. A new grocery store opened in our neighborhood and I tore up the key card because it asked where I was employed.

I interviewed for two positions early in the summer and did not get either job. That was an experience I had never had, but I was 52 years old and they were looking for a long-term commitment to work with young people. I interviewed for one position that was still not filled five years later.

In July I received a call from a friend who said there was an opening at NWTC where I had worked part time before moving to the Academy. I applied for the job, interviewed and was hired within a week. The description called for me to run workshops and assist older workers who had lost their jobs when companies closed.

I stood in front of the first group a month later and repeated with strong feeling. "And when one door closes, another one opens and I am proof that is true." I repeated that phrase for eleven years to people who had worked at Northwest Engineering, Diana Manufacturing, and the Boston Store among others, and when I retired in 2001, I received benefits I never would have had if I had gone to the new school. I still have strong friendships and luncheon dates with co-workers from both schools and I have totally forgiven that principal who did me a tremendous favor.

SJA

A TRIP TO KILN

It was spring, 1994, and Easter was in April, always a favorite month for spring break in the Florida Panhandle. We eagerly awaited our trip and even after twenty years the anticipation of snow-white sand and emerald colored water was no less exciting. The first twelve years were spent camped in Holiday Campground right on the Gulf of Mexico.

A group of Preble teachers and families started out on Holy Thursday, as early as we could get away, and usually set up by Friday night. In 1987, we moved down the road a mile to the Beach House condominiums. The old Tradewinds camper could no longer be trusted to make the 1200-mile trip. After Gene's retirement we extended our stay from a week to 10 days and finally two weeks.

We always celebrated Easter with the entire group and this year was no exception. Lisa and Zack flew into Fort Walton Beach Airport for a week's stay and we joined the Schmidts, Grahams, Eversols, Pirmans and their relatives, the Proctors and Kathy and Peggy Long. After the usual time spent walking on the shores of the Gulf and Choctawatchee Bay, men's golfing and ladies shopping, tanning and eating seafood, we made plans with Frank and Gerrie Pirman to drive to New Orleans to tour for a couple days on our way home.

Frank, reluctant to face facts, awoke to tell Gerrie that his hip was too painful for the walking we would do, and he was heading home for surgery so Gene and I set out on our own.

Approaching Kiln (pronounced Kill) on Highway 10, we found ourselves in need of gas and headed off to the hometown of the one-year wonder, Packer quarterback Brett Favre (pronounced Farve). Out of curiosity Gene asked the station attendant where Brett lived and she responded, "Brett who?" Hearing this, a co-worker volunteered that we were close and offered directions to his parent's home on Ervin Farve Road. Yup! That is what it said on the road sign. These people seem to have a hard time making up their minds.

Plans to do a quick drive-by turned into an adventure as we soon discovered that the road ended in their yard and in order to turn around we would have to wait for another Wisconsin car to move.

"Back up," I pleaded, embarrassed to be caught at such unabashed celebrity spying. "Too late," responded my husband as we watched a little lady standing nearby leaning on a cane, waving good-bye to the other car while motioning us to take its place. There was no polite escape.

Ilse French, better known as Meemaw, Brett's maternal grandmother, radiated Southern hospitality. She and her husband described as "a bit of a pirate" in an article we had just read in Sports

Illustrated, had operated a supper club in Pass Christian for years. After his death, she moved to a trailer home on the property of her daughter Bonita, and her husband, Erv, Brett's parents.

"Come on," she insisted. "I'll show you where we watch the Packer games," and we paraded past the tree where the familiar wooden Packer was swinging, toward the pool house that the favorite son had built for his family.

We strolled past the modest, red brick home where Brett had grown up. We would much later hear of the harrowing escape they made when Hurricane Katrina trapped them in the attic and they had to crawl through a window and swim for their lives to the second floor of the pool house.

Meemaw pointed across a narrow strip of water known as Rotten Bayou toward the woods that she explained shielded the home of the Brennans, owners of the famous New Orleans restaurant known for innovative menus and lavish breakfasts.

Entering the pool house, we found a collection of memorabilia including jerseys and pictures from Brett's football years. A hot tub sat in one corner and a modest grouping of chairs adorned the rest of the room. A large deck stood out over the bayou and we later read amusing stories of the antics of the Favres, including Deanna, and Brett's teammates who visited the area and were sometimes challenged to dive into the alligator infested water beneath the deck.

Meemaw confided that she no longer attended Brett's games. He was injured in the last game she saw and she felt she was bad luck. He disagreed but she was not about to change her mind. He was currently attending a mini camp in Arizona. The other family members were at work leaving her to provide hospitality to wandering snowbirds.

At Christmas time in 2003, when I was undergoing radiation treatment for breast cancer, our kids came home and by luck happened upon a book signing at Bay Park Square Mall.

Purchasing the Favre Family cookbook, Lisa told Bonita and her son and daughter about our trip to Kiln, bringing a look of consternation and an autograph that simply said, "Hope you enjoy the book! Hope you enjoyed your trip to Mississippi." It is signed Bonita, Brandy and Scott Favre.

THE BEST PARTY EVER

The merger of two daily newspapers, the Menominee Herald Leader and the Marinette Eagle Star brought about a big change in my brother Bob's life. The move from city editor to feature writer was unwelcome, and the philosophy of the new paper was different. He had covered the political campaign of Michigan Representative Bart Stupak, and when offered the opportunity to work as a press aide in his Washington office, he accepted. In-laws, Rick and Claudia Schoener, offered a room in their Reston, Virginia, townhouse and he moved in in the fall of 1995. As Bart would be running soon for a second term, Dina and the boys maintained their home in Menominee but when he was reelected, a decision had to be made.

Bill Clinton was also about to start his second term in January of 1997, and when I arrived home from work one Wednesday evening I received a call from Dina.

"Would you be interested in attending the inauguration?" she asked. "Bob will have to work but we can take part in the activities and he will join us when he can." We would be attending the Michigan Dinner Dance, not an official event attended by the Clintons, but she assured me it was "the hottest ticket in town."

Somewhat overwhelmed by the unexpected invitation, I told her I would talk to Gene and get back to her. Gene said he was not interested in going but he encouraged me to go and I crawled into bed to think…for about ten minutes. Then I called Dina back and said, "If I can get on the same plane you are on, I will come."

I was given permission to take off work and I called and booked my flight for Friday, January 17. Gene drove us to Austin Straubel and we flew to Detroit. A brief layover allowed us time for a glass of wine and a chat. Dina recommended that I turn my watch an hour ahead so that when we arrived in D.C. we would be on the correct time.

The Schoeners lived in a three-story condo in the community of Reston VA, designed to enable residents to live and work within walking distance. Rick was employed by the Department of Transportation and he, like Bob, traveled the belt line into the city each weekday. Claudia was an RN, working for a fertility clinic and would be on call all that weekend.

Saturday morning, I awoke in my comfortable bed, with a down filled comforter, and after preparing for the day, I opened the Washington Post to read the latest news on the Super Bowl. Green Bay would be playing New England in New Orleans. That news filled the pages of The Green Bay paper each day but much to my chagrin no mention was made in the nation's capital. I called Gene to express my dismay that here we did not exist.

After brunch, Bob, Dina and I drove to downtown Washington

where a variety of activities were planned across the mall. One of our goals was to see an Irish dance group but when we arrived they were just completing their performance. Bob had to return to Bart's office in Rayburn so Dina and I made our way back, killing time, and warming up in various museums. It was colder in Washington than it was in Green Bay!

We were to meet Bob and return to Claudia's by 4:30 but when we arrived he greeted us and showed us his watch, which read 5:30. Dina had changed watches, wearing one she had not turned ahead in Detroit. I never looked at mine.

That evening we dressed to attend a party sponsored by the Roemer Group, local political advisors hired to assist newcomers to congress. It was held in a beautiful three-story townhouse just off the Hill. The people who built it designed it to look like the wife's family home in Baltimore. They eventually moved across the street so they could "look at it".

Everyone was friendly and did their best to make us comfortable. It appeared that they were determined to convince Dina that Washington was a livable place and she would be welcome should she decide to make it her home.

Beginning with drinks in the library on the third floor we eventually moved to the second level, the kitchen and dining area of the house. There we indulged in salmon flown in from Alaska that morning and smoked by our host. A beautiful array of fresh fruit and cheeses were displayed on elaborate serving dishes along with other interesting finger foods. Original artwork inspired stimulating conversation. From there we made our way down to the first floor where a variety of desserts and coffees were served before the evening ended.

Sunday morning I again checked the Post that now acknowledged there would be a Super Bowl in New Orleans and we set out for the city to attend a brunch at the home of the press secretary to Michigan's Carl Levin. Here we were introduced to a group of friends and relatives of other Washington workers who had come to town for the party. Again they worked their magic on Dina who would see "real people" could and did live in or near the Capital. Another lovely old townhouse provided interesting chatter, mimosas and quiche. One of the guests, a relative of our hostess, had lived in Hawaii for twenty years and much to my surprise was acquainted with Judy and Ray Oda. Ray was a classmate of my husband at UW La Crosse and they had been our very gracious guides when we visited Oahu. He had gone back home to teach in his hometown and was an active member of his community.

After a few tourist stops at the Hercules sculpture and the new

FDR Memorial we headed back to Reston for dinner and a relaxing evening in Shoener's third floor theater watching the President's gala on a large screen TV.

Monday morning, January 20, 1998, brought a flurry of activity. Dina and I boarded the Metro to meet Bob who had driven in earlier. We climbed the steep steps at Capitol South as the escalator was not working. It was still bitter cold but the crowd seemed to exude warmth.

From where we stood we could see Hillary's coral dress and John Warner and Newt Gingrich's white hair. Microphones were set up all over the mall and the sound boomed over the heads of thousands of ticketed spectators who stretched behind us for blocks. The new president, William Jefferson Clinton, spoke positively of the challenges facing the twenty-first century.

After the swearing in, we were invited to lunch in Bart's office in Rayburn, and as I visited with his family, I discovered that these Michigan people were traveling to New Orleans to watch my Packers play. I somewhat disgruntledly had to acknowledge the privileges of holding office. Dina and I left early to find a spot to watch the parade. We saw bands, Barbara Walters, Hillary and Tipper Gore before decided to head back to meet Bob and return to Reston in time for Dina's hair appointment.

Later that evening escorted by Bob, dapper in Rick's tuxedo, we handed the car over to the valet parker and entered the Museum of American History. I wore a navy blue lace and chiffon floor length dress with blue patent leather shoes. Dina was lovely in her blue cocktail length dress.

It was all very exciting with elegant buffet tables featuring Michigan products, desserts as well as cocktail and coffee bars. We toured the Museum, looked at former first ladies' inaugural gowns, munched on oysters, tenderloin, turkey, pasta and lots of food made with cranberries, Michigan food products. Bob joined us for dinner in a room overlooking a spotlighted Washington Monument. It was so beautiful and a four-piece strings group played soft music while we visited and ate.

An assortment of musical groups played throughout the museum and I was sorry later that I missed Linda Carter. Wonder Woman was my favorite star when I was growing up.

Our $120 ticket entitled us to a gift bag with a silver picture frame engraved with the date and the occasion, a pen and a disposable camera. Dina and I had our picture taken with a cutout of the Clintons that a friend later thought was real.

As the party was ending and we waited for our car we were introduced to Rick's new boss, Department of Transportation

Secretary, Rodney Slater, and also shook hands with Michigan Senator Carl Levin who had just brought down Newt Ginrich for misappropriation of campaign funds. Everyone was flying high. We got home around 1 AM. We found out later that the actual inaugural balls were quite disorderly. They were served beer and chips and when it came time to leave, the coat check people became flustered and actually ran from their posts in tears, forcing ball goers to dig for their furs and topcoats. The Michigan dinner dance was surely the place to be!

On Tuesday, January 21, we took the Metro to Bart's office to get tickets to visit the Gingrich hearing in the House. There were big crowds and long lines and we got lost cutting through the Library of Congress on our way to the Capitol. We finally gave up and decided to visit the new Holocaust Museum. It was a good decision but the piles of suitcases left behind by victims on their way to the gas chamber brought tears. We were given a biography of one person to follow through timelines and I was grateful to find that mine survived. Students visiting were quiet and respectful and the tour ended in a meditation room where candles were lit for friends and family who did not.

After a final stop to meet my representative, Jay Johnson, we headed back to Reston and our final evening was spent in a chili bar with Bob, Peter Johnson and Dina.

Wednesday we arose at 4:30 AM and drove to Dulles to board our flight and I got home in time to unpack, dress and drag myself to work from 12:30 to 8:30.

It was humorous to read that evening's Press Gazette. Unlike the Post, it was filled with articles on the upcoming football game. On page seven I found a brief article describing the inauguration, the best party I ever attended.

Mary Lynn, Bob and Dina

THE THRILL OF VICTORY; THE ANONIMITY OF DEFEAT

We had worked our way to the front of the platform where we waited with some trepidation for the next train to arrive. We weren't sure whether the restless crowd behind us would shove us onto the tracks, or worse yet, some green and gold clad fan would throw himself under the wheels. It was Sunday, January 25, 1998, and the Green Bay Packers had just lost the Super Bowl.

What a week it had been! We had flown into Ontario, California, and headed for Escondido, current home of our son, Dan, and his wife Vickie. Tuned to a local station in our rental car we listened to the drive show DJ's ridiculing the Cheeseheads, the fat people from the Frozen Tundra, the Packer backers who were taking over San Diego.

We soon joined them flocking to Coronado Island and the Hotel Del. The first person we met on our way to the waterfront was the gentleman who sat behind us in Lambeau and loudly predicted every play. He was mostly wrong which drove everyone crazy, but we were happy to see a familiar face.

We mingled at the marina, drummed with a salsa band at the Marriott, rode the trolley to Old Town and totally took over the Gaslight District. We skipped the Favre family party. Word had it that you waited in a long line to pay $25 to wait even longer to buy a brat and a beer. Instead we walked the parameter of QUALCOMM Stadium chatting with RV campers who had driven across country to cheer on the Pack. We snapped a picture of a handsome, young San Diego cop who had corralled a stray cow kite obviously flown in from the Midwest. That was our son, Dan Hall. Each night we returned to the apartment to listen to the news and watch the frenzy build.

Saturday, on a whim, we followed a van adorned with the familiar green and gold logo and found ourselves at Torrey Pines, famous for its golf tournaments and current home of the team from Wisconsin. There we chatted with Herman Reckleburg, a friend and member of the Packer Board, and his daughter Roxie, and checked the players coming and going.

We also spotted Sam Ramsden, our self-appointed ticket finder, and pushed Vickie in front of his slow moving car to ask how the search was coming. The Packer trainer, and friend of Dan's from UW La Crosse, assured us that it was looking good.

Finally it was game day and at 9:30 AM, five hours before kickoff, we got the call. Tickets, held by the team for unexpected VP's had been released and employees who had requested extra were notified. Sam got four and we donned our gear and headed for Qualcomm to mingle with the crowd.

Not everyone had been as fortunate as we were and two young cops who also stayed with Dan received an offer of $7000 for their tickets. Sam said the tickets, which cost us $300 each, were ours to do with as we wished. Our wish was to experience a repeat of the New Orleans Super Bowl XXXI, but it was not to be and the underdogs came out on top.

This is the lesson we learned on that sunny January day. Vince Lombardi once said, "There are only two places-- first and last" and now we knew what he meant. We returned to the apartment and turned on the television in time to watch the Broncos fans celebrate by overturning cars in downtown Denver. There was no mention of the team they had competed against. After a week of being the media darlings, the Green Bay Packers and their fans had ceased to exist.

Hawleys and Halls at Qualcomm Stadium

IS A PICTURE REALLY WORTH A THOUSAND WORDS?

In December, 2007, I fulfilled a dream when we flew with our daughter and her family to our son's home in California to celebrate Christmas. On December 26, we dressed everyone in assorted shades of brown and trouped to Picture People in Temecula's Mall. Most of us smiled, none of the kids cried and much to my delight we found a picture we could all be happy with. The Hall Christmas card for 2009 was taken care of and the rather pricey 27 x 17 inch frame and matting that I chose was suitable for hanging in my living room. Having read way too many English novels I even imagined some future ancestor gazing up and saying, "They were a pleasant looking group....that Brown Family!"

It was the following March and my husband and I were basking in the sun at Happy Trails resort in Surprise, AZ, when we received a phone call. "Hey, Grandma, remember when we all got in the Sequoia and Dan looked around and said, 'We could get one more person in here?' Vickie asked. Well, yes I did, but I just thought he was commenting on the size of the car.

Then Carley asked, "Grandma, can you buy us a new stroller? My mom threw the old one out." I had assumed she was tired after walking a couple miles to the grocery story and Starbucks.

But no, that was not the case. The Halls were expecting an addition to their family. It was as big of a surprise to them as it was to us. We would be welcoming a fifth grandchild in September. Did I jump for joy? Did I scream my congratulations? 'No!" I shouted into the phone. "My picture is outdated and no one has even seen it!" Well sure, I was glad to be a grandma again but the Brown family had never made it unto a Christmas card!

We got together the following summer and took one picture but Zack and Tallen were missing. We have a shot of Grandma and Grandpa with the California girls and one with the Illinois boys, but the odds were not good that that ancestor would have a chance to gaze up fondly at a complete picture of a family dressed in brown or any other color.

Finally, in the summer of 2005, we gathered at Lisa's in Chicago to celebrate the Fourth of July. We donned various shades of gray and traveled once again to Picture People.

While driving to Lindbergh Field in San Diego recently for a return trip home, my son and I talked about the miracle that is Kami. I reminded him that we had had one daughter and then lost three baby girls, one full term, due to RH factor incompatibility. We adopted him when he was one week old. So much sorrow resulted in so much joy! He thought momentarily and then looked at me and said, "So that is

68

the reason we have three little girls!"

Sometimes just ten words are worth more than one picture.

"THAT GRAY FAMILY"

Top Row: Zack Gutkowski, Dan, Mary Lynn and Gene Hall, Tallen Mahaffey

Bottom Row: Sydney, Vickie and Kami Hall, Lisa Mahaffey and Carley Hall,

Jake Mahaffey

THE DAY I MADE A DIFFERENCE

For years I had read stories in People Magazine about projects that individuals and groups accomplished on the nationally declared "Make a Difference Day". I would fantasize about organizing co-workers. We were a huge organization and together we could really make headlines. Maybe the members of my church, the Social Welfare Committee, or the Altar Rosary Society, would choose to reach out to someone in need in mid-October. But here I was, retired for nine years, and still just reading about what others had done.

I am not sure what turned me on this particular day, but as I neared the completion of a three-mile hike, I found myself in front of the Red Cross center on the corner of Deckner and Danz. An eight-gallon blood donor before undergoing treatment for breast cancer, I had not given for several years. Thinking that this might be a good start to making a difference, I stopped in and explained my circumstances to the lady behind the desk. I could even do apheresis now. Instead of drawing whole blood, they take out the platelets and return the rest. You can give more often but it involves a time commitment I was unable to make while working.

" I'll call Madison and ask what they prefer that you do," the woman promised. "We will call you soon." I barely made it through my kitchen door and the phone was ringing. Only six percent of the population has an A negative blood type so I have always been quite popular at the Red Cross.

Having made an appointment, I sat down with a cup of coffee only to spot a sheet of paper that I had picked up at the Humane Society a couple weeks ago. Driving home from Bay Beach, my daughter and grandson who were visiting from Illinois, asked to stop at the shelter to check out a cat sale they were advertising. While they fawned over every available animal, my husband and I looked over a brochure regarding foster care. There is a great need in the summer as strays are dropping litters all over town. We had pets for years but because we now traveled so much, we could not do that.

We had not acted upon the idea but because this was my day to do something different, I filled it out and dropped it off figuring that with fall approaching it would be a good time to cuddle up with a kitten on a cool evening.

The next day, still summer with the thermostat approaching 87 degrees, I received a call from Tanya, the foster coordinator. "Could you come and pick up a family as soon as possible?" she asked. I have since learned that the correct response to this question is, "How many?" but I did not know the first time around. I was soon stumbling to my car barely able to lift a carrier holding a mom and six kittens. Over the next month, Holly, LeBron, Jake, identical twins,

Finn and Fang, and their sole sister Lady Gaga, redecorated the house. Confined to the sun porch and back bathroom, they unrolled toilet paper, rearranged decorations and carried on continuous wrestling tournaments for our entertainment and for those who dared to visit. It was literally a zoo from morning till night when they finally curled up in a pile in the carrier, usually on top of Mom.

As each kitten weighed in at two pounds, we returned them to the shelter to be neutered and offered for adoption. Everyone, including Mom, found forever homes. Since that time we have nursed and socialized Squeak, Kate and Will, Rose and Raji, Foster and Lambeau. Finally, Stache would greet me each morning and insist upon helping me brush my teeth and comb my hair.

In September of 2011, my husband suffered a stroke. At the time we had Matty (think Clay Matthews) and for the thirty days that I sat with him at the hospital, Gene would turn to me and ask, "You aren't going to take that cat back are you?" I knew our travel times would now be limited so he came home to a scraggily kitten who crawled on his lap as they both napped. That was almost eight years ago and she has grown considerably and is a pretty Torby, a tortoiseshell and tabby mix. She is my company since my husband passed away last spring.

I know she cares about me. I went to the computer to check the results after a particularly important election. Disappointed, I returned to bed and shed a few quiet tears. Next thing I knew Matty crawled up to lie on my chest and place her paw on my cheek.

During one trip to the Red Cross they noticed that my blood pressure was rising, a problem I had not experienced in the past, and I was required to take medication to remedy that. I thought Make a Difference Day meant improving the lives of others but now I know that both actions I took on that summer day have made a significant difference in mine.

Foster Fun in Gene's slipper

There were days when my husband and I would talk about events that occurred in his life. Reminiscing seemed to help his memory so I decided one New Years Day when we were confined to the house to write a story that he remembered from many years before.

REMEMBERING THE CIGAR BOWL

When John Knispel became my brother Bob Meissner's football coach at Menominee High School my mother liked to tell people that he played in the "Tobacco Bowl" with her son-in-law. In reality, Gene and John played for LaCrosse State Teachers College in the Cigar Bowl on January 1, 1951.

1950 had been a good year for the La Crosse Indians. They drew record crowds for their nine season victories and they scored 344 points while holding opponents to 62 making them the highest scoring undefeated eleven in the nation. The college newspaper published the headline, Indians Await Call to Arms While Department Ponders Over Which Bowl.

They received an invitation to the Corn Bowl to be played on Thanksgiving in Bloomington, IL, and a feeler group attempted to establish a Dairy Bowl with St. Norbert as the opponent. When the Cigar Bowl bid came Coach Clark Van Galder accepted the game to be played on January 1.

The bowl featured small college teams and was played in

Tampa from 1946 to 1954. Sponsored by a local Shrine Temple, it was a fundraiser for their children's hospital. It was named for the industry that had been a major factor in Tampa's growth at the turn of the century.

Practicing football in Wisconsin in December presented a challenge and with the financial backing of many loyal fans, a contingent of 60 boarded a Captial Airlines DC4 on December 27. The idea of a warm climate was appealing and along with the band and cheerleaders, a large group of fans boarded buses. Driving straight through they arrived On Thursday, December 28.

Coach Van Galder was a well-liked, somewhat fiery coach who pleased crowds as he paced the sidelines shouting out orders. He gave Gene, a life-long nickname when he would shout, "Gunner, Hall, gunner!" Seventy years later there were still those who called him Gunner. The coach also sent his son to make sure the former East High track member was awake for afternoon practice.

La Crosse was expecting a challenging passing game from the opponent's quarterback, but the Indians intercepted five times and the half time score was 21-7. Ace Loomis, who later played for the Packers, set a new bowl record scoring five touchdowns.

With a win assured La Crosse players, including 12 graduating seniors, began entertaining the crowd. On the final TD, instead of kicking the extra point, John Knispel, always a bit of a practical joker when it came to play calling, threw the ball. The entire defense rushed John leaving Gene alone in the end zone to catch the pass.

The team and its fans celebrated. Emptying the floors of the Hotel Floridian the fifty-member band marched down Cass Street playing "On Wisconsin". Homecoming Queen Peg Vickery, unprepared for such an occasion, donned a lovely pink formal borrowed from a minister's wife. Also attending a gathering at the hotel and hearing of Peg's dilemma, she insisted that her dress be worn in the parade. One paper shared that "the crowd liked her looks and she did not have to step aside for any southern belle." Peg also remembered that the bus was so loud on the way home she could not hear for two weeks.

A reunion held in 1991 coincided with homecoming weekend. Gene and I were invited to march onto the field at the halftime of the LaCrosse "Eagles" game escorting our son, Dan. He was a senior at the school representing the Political Science Program. It was a proud moment for both father and son.

The following is a memoir told in the first person by Gene four months after his stroke.

AND TO THINK THAT I SAW IT ON JACKSON STREET

The little pickup truck often passed me as I walked to St. John's School. Al Schneider, a neighbor from Van Buren Street, was beginning his day making deliveries for Schilling Fish. His son, Don, five at the time, along with the other neighbors, the Gays, Kalinosky's, and the Quatsoe's headed as I did for their respective schools. The neighborhood is now considered inner city and our house along with others has been torn down. At the time it was populated by growing families whose children would go on to make significant contributions to Green Bay.

A life-long resident of Oconto, my father moved our family to the big city in June of 1941, to accept a position at Hudson Sharp. Finding employment had been a challenge in Oconto during the depression years and he had held a variety of jobs hoping to remain in the area. He maintained machinery at a knitting mill that ultimately closed. He bought a truck and traveled to farms grinding grain for local farmers and he continued to repair sewing machines on the side. Dad served as clerk of courts for a couple years and also managed a Deep Rock station on Superior Street. Finally, with two children in elementary school, Dad decided that the future was not in

77

Oconto and we moved leaving behind family on both sides. This was especially difficult for my mother who longed to pack up the car and head North every weekend.

We settled into a rental house at 234 S. Jackson and I was welcomed to the neighborhood by Tom Gay, one of eight boys whose family lived behind us on Stuart Street. He led me to a small, sandy plot of land across from St. John's church. I chose to attend St. John's school, run by the Sisters of St. Joseph of Carondolet for eighth grade. That decision was made mainly because of a big man, Father Al Hietpas, who could be spotted on the playground shooting baskets or playing baseball with the kids. On one occasion I recall him hitting a baseball through a school window and pleading with us not to tell the nuns, although I suspect he soon confessed.

Within a year we purchased a home on South Irwin and my mother finally accepted the move. My father traveled for the company and she made friends with women in the neighborhood, shopped at four tiny stores within a couple blocks and I moved to Washington Junior and East High. Because high school graduates were being drafted into WW2, I was able to spend two summers of my high school years employed as a play leader at St. John's Park.

The old neighborhood, and those living in it, continued to grow. Don Quatsoe would move on to eventually become the warden of the Green Bay Correctional Institute. The Gays finally added a baby girl to their family and my friend, Tom, moved to the West Coast to settle. Norb Kalinosky and I both chose the field of education and he served as Vice-Principal of Preble High School where I taught for thirty-two years. And then there were the Schneiders.

I had picked up the Green Bay Press Gazette that Saturday, January 14, 2012, and read the front page obituary of Don Schneider. I suspect the Jackson neighborhood survivors of that period may also share the memory of his father's first truck. Barber, Connie Lotto, had recently told me that Al continually collected used truck parts…tires and all the rest. I am not sure if that is how he did it, but that one small truck grew into a fleet of 9,773 tractors, and 32,108 trailers, recognized world wide by their pumpkin orange color.

Don eventually took over and it evolved into a three billion-dollar industry with more than 18,000 employees worldwide. Just one little pickup truck….and to think that I saw it on Jackson Street!

Gene Hall as told to Mary Lynn Hall, January 2012

FIGHTING THE WAR AT FORT SHERIDAN

When Gene Hall signed up for a stint in the Army the war had just ended and so had his memorable high school athletic years. While archrival Green Bay West prevailed in the inter-city football competition that year, Green Bay East had dominated in basketball and finished the 1946 season in first place. The season ended early because the school district did not allow the two high schools to compete in the state tournament in Madison.

Gene worked through the summer on construction jobs with friend Rich Brosig and played baseball with the highly competitive Cobb's Bread team. In October he put away the work clothes, gloves and bats and traveled to Chicago with a couple of his classmates to enlist in the Army. After passing his physical, his options for training schools were limited so he chose the closest to home and headed for Fort Sheridan where he would enroll in Cook and Baker's School.

Shortly after arriving on base, Gene noticed postings asking for volunteers to play on the Cook and Baker's school basketball team or on the all-base team. Gene's superior was a basketball fan and asked the new soldier to drive him to observe the games. Opting for latter, ultimately known as "The Ramblers" and coached by player coach

Wally Pippin of Lake Forest, he boarded buses and traveled the area competing against Milwaukee industrial leagues as well as local colleges including Lake Forest and Milwaukee Teacher's College. This was without ever having gone through basic training.

A barracks orderly by day, Gene's job was to find 10 men to clean a day room and he was then free to meet his teammates to practice and compete. And what interesting teammates they were! From 1945 to 1947 the Ramblers won 58 out of 63 games mainly because of three players, Boryla, Melchiorre and Mann.

Vince Boryla had played two seasons for the Irish in 1944-45 and led the team in scoring with 643 points in 41 games. He was the first Notre Dame player to wear an Olympic basketball jersey in the 1948 London games, helping the US team roll over France to an easy gold medal in the final of eight games. He was also affiliated with the Denver Nuggets AAU team. A native of East Chicago, Indiana, Vince enlisted in the Army following his two years of college.

Two other members of the team would become famous for their skills as Bradley University players but infamous for becoming involved in scandal.

On July 24, 1951, Gene's former teammates, Gene Melchiorre, a 5'8" native of Joliet, IL, and his buddy Bill Mann, along with four college teammates, admitted taking bribes from professional gamblers to shave points to hold down scores in two games. "Squeak" Melchiorre was named an All-American at the end of the season, but because of the accusations he became an outcast. Many Peorians, and the school itself, stood up to pressure, and refused to hang his jersey in the gym with the other All-Americans. As first overall pick in the 1951 draft, he was chosen by the Baltimore Bullets but he never played a professional game due to his unfortunate choices.

When basketball season ended and no further threats of a foreign invasion surfaced, Gene went on to play first base on the baseball team. He and other servicemen caught trains to attend free White Sox games in Chicago. Unlike the Cubs who charged admission, the Sox let them in without paying. On occasion he was able to hitch a ride home with his boss, Major Pitlack, head of the Cook and Baker's school, who just happened to be from Green Bay.

All of this earned him the GI bill that helped pay his college tuition (which was about $50) and provided an allowance of $36 a month. Not bad for a bit of fun and a brush with the famous and infamous.

One final story is added because I know of nowhere else to publish it and it is too good to pass up. A high school friend of Gene's, sailed the Chicago to Mackinac race 18 years and when he told me the following tale, I asked him to write it with me. I spoke with a number of people from the hotel and the historical society on the island and no one admits to remembering this incident …but I don't doubt for a moment that it happened.

WHO STOLE THE BELL FROM THE GRAND HOTEL?

Menominee Michigan is a boating community. On summer nights our large, nervous collie climbed onto our laps and whined as the starter pistols fired to begin Thursday night sailboat races at the marina. In the 50s a July weekend found us watching participants of the Chicago to Mackinac Race anchor and prepare for the "100 miler" that would take place the next day. What a thrill to watch boats from "the big race" sail into our harbor! We shouted out the names as they approached and picked our favorites to cheer on. Some them were locals like the Derusha's and the Higley's.

The first Mac, in 1898, saw five boats make their way 333 miles from the Chicago Yacht Club to the island in the Straits of Mackinac which divide Upper and Lower Michigan. The war brought cancellation for several years but since 1921 it has run each year and is recognized as one of the most prestigious sailing races in the world. After I married and moved to Green Bay I retained an interest in the

"Mac" and I eagerly searched for results in the papers. And then I met Adolph. Ade, a friend of my new husband, was a member of the "Guernsey Kids," a Green Bay East High group who in the late 40's gathered at the Guernsey Dairy owned by one of the fathers. It was never made clear to me just what went on there but I suspect beer and cards may have been part of the picture. We had reunions regularly and the "Kids" returned from wherever they had moved....several from Chicago. Ade, a graduate engineer from UW Madison, was one of those. Upon learning that he was involved with sailing my favorite race, I looked forward to hearing his latest story and he never failed to come up with a good one. He crewed for at least 18 races but there is one tale I never tired of hearing. I have asked many times that we

 write it and finally this year he agreed to allow me to do so. I think I convinced him that the statute of limitations has expired.

Ade is not sure of the year when he and Roman "Brick", co-owners of the schooner Happy Holiday, along with five additional crew members, set sail from Chicago. It was probably in the early 60s. As he describes it, outside of an occasional blow, most years sailing the

race is "a cake walk" and that year was one of those. Arriving at Mackinac Island somewhere in the middle of the pack, they tied up and did what sailors finishing the race usually do. Ade, along with Fritz, one of the crew, headed out for some liquid relaxation. Rejecting the most popular spots, like The Pink Pony, the two men walked to the golf course snack shop adjoining the island's most famous landmark, the Grand Hotel.

View of the Grand Hotel from the harbor

Feeling a little regretful that another race had passed and they still had no trophy to show for their efforts, the two launched a plan to find their own, namely a bell on the grounds of the hotel. Using a hefty wrench, they easily dismounted the 50-pound relic and hastily returned to the ship where they stowed it under a dock above the water line. It wasn't long before the loss was discovered and searchers began questioning visitors to the island. False leads were established, namely the report of a young couple, with children, who had "suspiciously" been seen in the area but then hastily sailed from the harbor. The bell was reputed to have come from a famous battleship, certainly upping its value, although nothing can be found to establish that as a fact. To be safe, under cover of dark, the culprits wrapped their trophy in a sail bag and using a small boat moved it to a more obscure site along the shoreline. When the unsuspecting partner departed and it was time for the crew to make the return sail to Chicago, they recovered their prize and stowed it below.

A false sense of security set in on the trip back and they went so far as to exhibit the bell on the foredeck even as they pulled into ports along the lower Michigan coast, but a warning that word was out to search for the bell sent it once again into hiding.

Back in Illinois it took up residence all winter in the living room of Ade's Evanston apartment. Perhaps tiring of the dust it was gathering, or possibly feeling a twinge of guilt and regret, the culprits packed up the treasure one more time. Transporting it to UPS, they asked to have it boxed and shipped back to the Grand Hotel. Unbelievably, no questions were asked, no names were taken, and until now few people knew who stole the bell from the Grand Hotel and returned it C.O.D.

(As I was writing this I opened the local paper to read that Adolph passed away Easter week of 2019).

ACKNOWLEDGEMENTS

I would like to thank all of the friends, neighbors and co-workers who have been a part of our days for almost 60 years in Green Bay. Gene's family, the Paulson's have filled our lives with love and provided wonderful holiday food and fun.

My family suffered a second, heartbreaking loss when my sister-in-law, died in 2018 within a month of Gene. The times we traveled to visit with Dina and Bob, in Menominee and then in Annapolis, were so memorable for us and for our kids.

Thanks to everyone who helped me "remember" correctly and thanks to dear friend Mary Lee who always encourages me and especially to my daughter who designed my cover and contributed a great deal of time to the creation of this book.

Finally the kids, and their families can get ready for another Christmas present. Kami took my first book to school in CA to read sections to her class. How is that for encouragement!

DEDICATION

This book is dedicated to my loving husband Gene who provided his family with a lifetime of happiness and a world of adventure in his own quiet way till he passed on May 21, 2018.

ABOUT THE AUTHOR

Mary Lynn Meissner Hall has moved on from A TALE OF TWIN CITIES: GROWING UP IN MENOMINEE and

NEXT STOP: GREEN BAY continues her memoires. A degree in English from Mount Mary University and an MS in Educational Psychology from UW Milwaukee plus advanced certification in religious education, contribute to her lifetime of employment and enjoyment as a wife, mother, teacher and counselor.

Made in the USA
Coppell, TX
15 March 2020

16887481R00049